Ray Manley's THE FINE ART OF NAVAJO WEAVING

Collection and Text by Steve Getzwiller

Spider Rock in Canyon de Chelly is the mythical home of Spider Woman.

"The Fine Art of Navajo Weaving" today has become just that, a fine art. With each passing year the general quality continues to improve. More and more Navajo women, and recently several men, are establishing well deserved reputations for their proficiency at the loom. These weavers continually strive to perfect their skills while experimenting with new ideas and design concepts. The last ten years have brought a new prosperity to the art. It is now possible for a top weaver to earn a comfortable living working on a full time basis. This was not the case a few years ago. Until now, and still only for a few, weaving did not afford more than a supplemental income.

The refinements in Navajo weaving today have not gone unnoticed. Serious collectors of these textiles are continually seeking and finding ever finer examples. Museums are recognizing the changes and the necessity for updating existing collections. In general, more and more people who in the past only thought of "Indian Rugs" as a "curio craft item" are now beginning to take notice.

The quality of some weaving has now attained its highest level since the pre-Bosque Redondo "Classic Period." It has taken more than one hundred years and the introduction of progessively finer quality wools to accomplish this, but it is now a fact. I personally know several dozen artists who are capable of producing comparable to finer work as that of the "golden era of Navajo Weaving," and do when compensated for the additional time and effort. The problem is that Navajo weaving in general remains one of the poorest paying Indian art forms.

This uniquely Navajo art is probably not in any current danger of being lost. It has become too much a part of the culture. Many younger women are learning to weave more out of a sense of pride in their heritage than anything else. Whether or not they will continue to practice it is another matter. It is not unusual for me to see a woman, whose work normally commands as much as several thousand dollars, making a saddle blanket for a son or relative, or experimenting with a small rug in a twill weave, just for fun.

(continued on page 48)

Spider Woman instructed the Navajo women how to weave on a loom which Spider Man told them how to make. The crosspoles were made of sky and earth cords, the warp sticks of sun rays, the heddles of rock crystal and sheet lightning. The batten was a sun halo, white shell made the comb. There were four spindles: one stick of zigzag lightning with a whorl of cannel coal; one a stick of flash lightning with a whorl of turquoise; a third had a stick of sheet lightning with a whorl of abalone; a rain streamer formed the stick of the fourth, and its whorl was white shell.

—Navajo Legend—

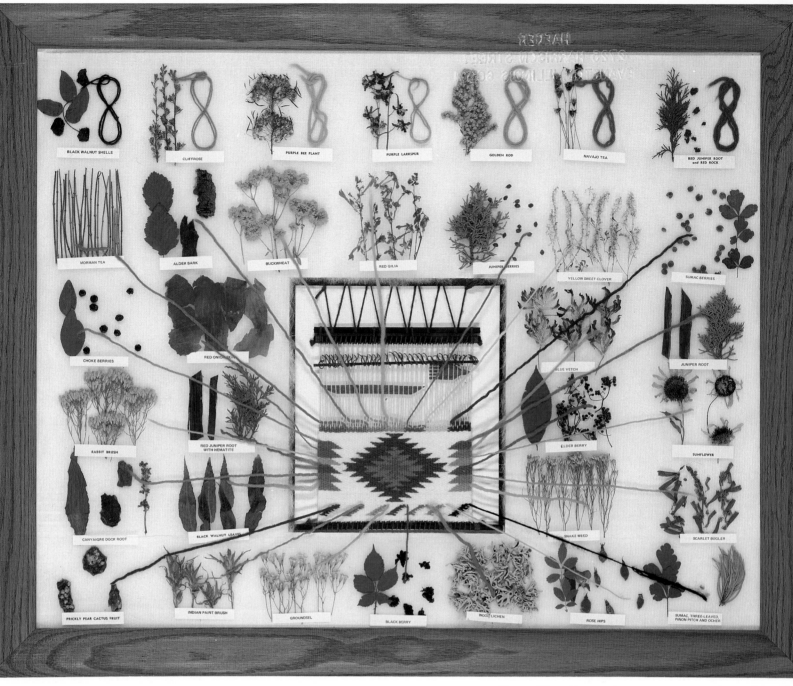

Framed Dye Chart by Isabell Deshinne, Window Rock Are

Dye Chart

The vegetal dyeing of wool is an involved procedure requiring considerable time and preparation. There is wood to be chopped for the fire; water to be drawn into barrels from community wells; both require hauling, sometimes for great distances. A Navajo weaver thinks nothing of driving and walking all day to locate the plants she knows will produce the best results.

Once prepared into yarn, the wool must be thoroughly washed and rinsed at least twice. She may use enamel pots only in which to soak and boil her wool and dye stuffs. Pots of tin, aluminum, or metal will produce a chemical reaction with the acid which develops in the dye bath by the fermenting dye stuffs, thus altering the color.

For the darker tones it is sometimes necessary to soak and ferment dye stuffs up to three or four weeks, with shorter periods producing progessively lighter hues. A great deal of time is involved in reboiling and dyeing, if it is necessary to achieve the desired color. It is almost impossible for a weaver to match colors in additional dye baths, so she must be certain of dyeing enough wool at one time in order to complete her rug without any color changes.

Once dyed, the yarn must again be thoroughly rinsed in order to achieve uniform color. Much care is taken in the drying process, so that water and dye will not collect at one end of the skein of wool, thus altering the color.

The same plants gathered at different times of the year will produce varying colors. Those gathered in summer and early fall will give richer colors, while those gathered in winter and early spring will produce lighter tones.

In short there are many involved steps in this process. When you stop to consider the number of blended colors in one Wide Ruins or Burntwater piece, they truly are a work of art. I'll never cease to be amazed and impressed at the determination of the Navajo weaver who digs up tree roots for their fragile inner bark, and gathers small bits of lichen from rocks in her constant quest for color.

Pine Springs

Evelyn Yazzie / 36" × 48"

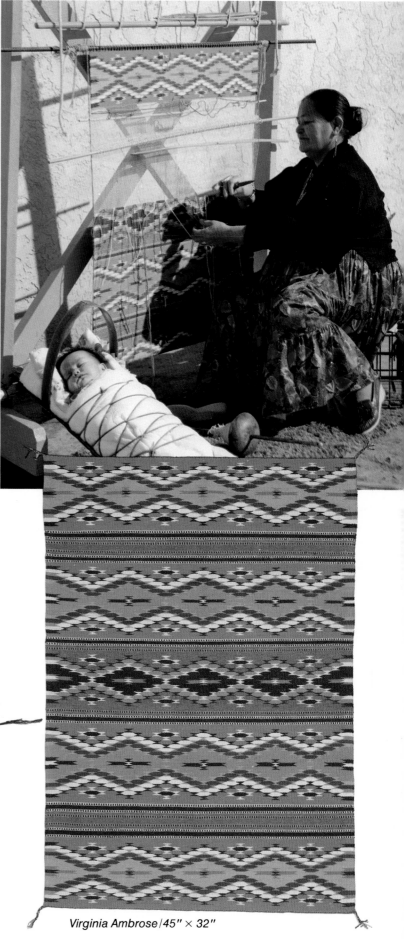

Virginia Ambrose weaving in the afternoon sun with her granddaughter.

If there is a distinguishable difference in weaving of the Pine Springs area from Wide Ruins, it lies in the subtle use of color. There is a tendency towards the use of slightly darker color combinations in the Pine Springs types. The most noticeable differences, however, lie in the slightly bolder design elements used in this Pine Springs weaving.

Cora Baldwin / 30" × 42"

Virginia Ambrose / 45" × 32"

Master Weaver–Ellen Smith working at her loom.

Wide Ruins

Annie Tsosie/36″ × 51″

Ellen Smith/42″ × 58″

Agnes Smith

This area's weavings are the most refined of the vegetal dye types. They incorporate intricate serrate design elements of soft, pastel earth tones of native plant dyes intermittently with solid bands of color. Outlining the main design bands or in alternating stripes are intricately woven ticking and beaded designs, these giving the impression of fine embroidery. Small amounts of natural white and gray wools are used within the designs to emphasize the vegetal dye combinations.

In recent years the design elements have become increasingly complex and the dye palette more extensive. Constant experimentation has resulted in the ability to achieve almost any hue imaginable. For these reasons they are highly desirable to collectors.

Nellie Roan/48" × 60"

Nellie Roan

In this example, the weaver has intentionally produced a Burntwater style of rug woven complete with tassels, and three dimensionally within a Wide Ruin design. It reflects not only her ability as a master weaver but her artistic ingenuity as well.

Mary Jane Barker

This rug illustrates very well the adaptability of the weaver to outside influences. The three main design bands are from examples of embroidery patterns taken from a copy I supplied of H. P. Mera's book Pueblo Indian Embroidery. I have also supplied several weavers in this area with booklets on plains Indian beadwork patterns; both styles lend themselves very well to this type of weaving design.

Mary Jane Barker/36" × 48"

Burntwater

Burntwater rugs are a relatively new development in contemporary weaving. They have evolved from the desire of a few innovative weavers to produce an elaborate, bordered geometric design such as those seen in the finer Ganado and Two Grey Hills area rugs, but in their native vegetal dyes. These weavings met with great success for the traders of this area, therefore they were encouraged. However, there are still relatively few of these weavers who are willing to assume the additional effort necessary to learn different techniques from the traditional Wide Ruins style. These qualities have made the Burntwater rug more desirable to knowledgeable collectors.

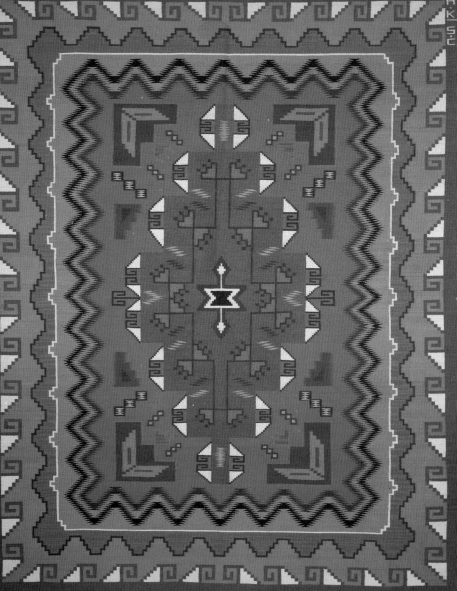

Helen Kirk–Sadie Curtis/5' × 7'

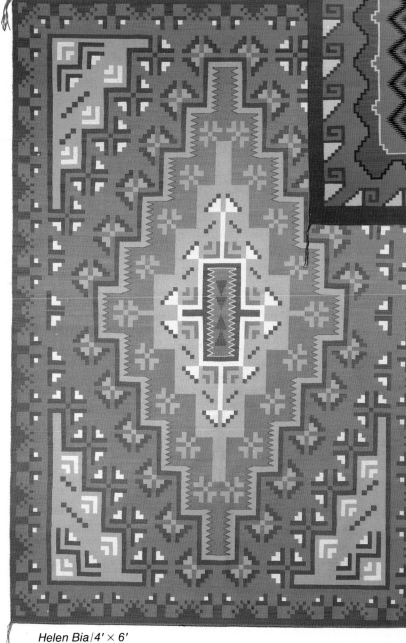

Helen Bia/4' × 6'

The Burntwater by Sadie Curtis and Helen Kirk was turning out so well that I suggested that they sign it with their initials as an artist would a painting. The idea took. Sadie and several other weavers now sign everything they weave with their initials woven in one corner.

Philomena Yazzie/42" × 66"

Kathy Lee (23 years old)/36" × 48"

The above rug by Philomena Yazzie was purchased by the Denver Art Museum. The museum has recently updated their contemporary collection with some very outstanding examples.

The Burntwater textiles woven by Kathy Lee (right) and Virginia Yazzie (below) are exceptional. Both women have been weaving since their teens and are now only in their very early twenties. These girls are going places!

Virginia Yazzie/3' × 5'

Celia Begay/3' × 5'

Betty B. Roan/36" × 54"

Ellen Smith

Nellie Roan

Marie Begay

Betty B. Roan

Annie Tsosie

Mary Jane Barker

Alice Balone, Sadie Curtis, and myself

The textiles shown on these pages represent a significant achievement in contemporary Navajo weaving. It is a combination of the talents of six of the most talented vegetal dye artists of the Wide Ruins area, and the weaving and design abilities of two of the finest weavers of the Ganado region.

There are twenty-five subtly blended vegetal dye colors involved in this weaving. They represent some of the more desirable hues which the six ladies to the left are most noted for. This dye information is generally shared only with family members and no one else, which, by the way, is another reason for much of the experimentation. Some colors are considered by some weavers to be family hallmarks.

Over a period of several years, I established the confidence necessary to commission the preparation of the wool used in this rug. The actual preparation time required approximately six months. These ladies would never consider doing this for someone they did not know well and trust.

I commissioned Sadie Curtis to do the weaving of this piece because of her outstanding design and technical ability. Together with her aunt, Alice Balone, and in approximately six months of weaving time, they completed this masterpiece. It is exceptionally large, and is finely woven for a rug of its type, for most pieces do not exceed 3′ × 5′, or 4′ × 6′.

In the scene below, some of the artists responsible for the dyed wool inspect the fruits of their labor for the first time. They greatly admired and enthusiastically discussed the piece, and each was justifiably proud of her own contribution to it.

Dye artists inspecting rug for the first time.

Burntwater by Alice Balone—Sadie Curtis/6' × 9'

Klagetoh

Approximately ten miles north of Wide Ruins is the small community of Klagetoh, English translation for which is "Hidden Springs." This area's rugs are generally considered to be a sub-type of the Ganado rugs from farther north. They are similar in that they have bordered geometric designs comprised of aniline red and black dyes, and use various shades of natural gray wools.

Klagetoh area rugs will have a predominantly natural gray background, with red, black, and white geometric design highlights. Predominant red backgrounds are the rule with the Ganado style. Also, the border designs of today's Klagetoh rugs tend to be less elaborate than those of the Ganado area.

Emma Lee/50" × 70"

Canyon de Chelly

Maxine Lee/3′ × 5′

Evelyn Yazzie/3′ × 4′

Elizabeth Bennally/3′ × 4′

Annie Tsosie

The example of Annie F. Tsosie's weaving (right) illustrates the influence and proximity of the Wide Ruins style. Many of the weavers of this area do both the Klagetoh and Wide Ruins type weaving, both in the aniline and vegetal dyes. This particular piece was a special order.

Annie Tsosie/28″ × 48″

Alice Begay

This very fine example by Alice Begay is particularly unusual because of its use of natural brown wool in place of the gray, a combination which is not often seen, but it is very attractive and effective.

Alice Begay/4′ × 5′

Ganado

The Ganado area is located nearly in the geographic center of the Navajo Reservation, and has long been the center for the "Ganado Red" type of Navajo rug. This style of weaving was established prior to 1900 by the famous trader, Don Lorenzo Hubbell. Originally, the bold cross and diamond motifs were adaptations of colors and designs taken from the earlier wearing blankets of the Navajos at a time when the traders in other areas of the Navajo Reservation were encouraging rug designs with an obvious "oriental influence" for the eastern market. Mr. Hubbell emphasized the use of the older elements, the result being a very pleasing, and to most laymen, a more "traditional Indian rug." His sphere of influence extended over a very broad area. At one time he owned and operated fourteen trading posts in the central and western regions of the Reservation. This, combined with a long business relationship with the Fred Harvey Co., explains the broad exposure and early popularity of this style of rug.

In 1967 the trading post was purchased by the National Park Service from Dorothy Hubbell. It is now maintained as a National Historic site and is still the trading center for the area.

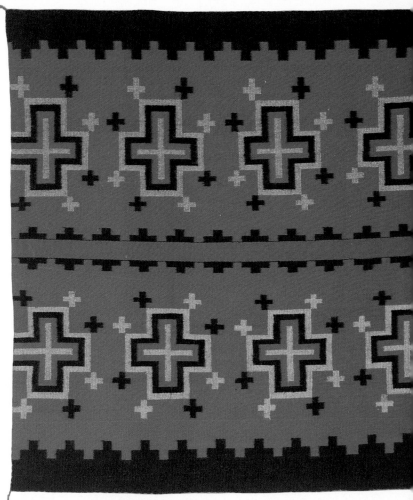

Mae Jim/10' × 15'

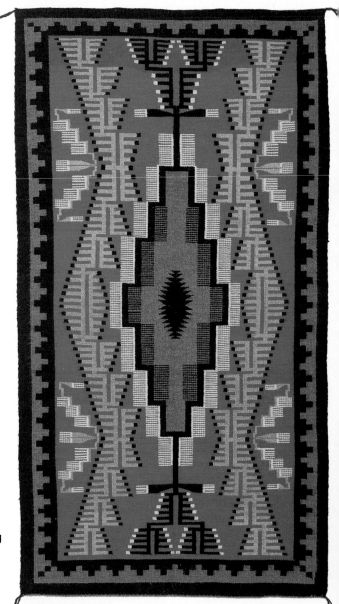

Louise Begay/48" × 66"

Mae Jim

Special attention was needed to begin work on this very large rug. First, six-inch steel pipe and four-by-twelve inch beams were used in the loom construction to insure maximum control in weaving a rug of this size. Also, it was necessary to remove a portion of the ceiling in order to accommodate the loom. She estimates that it will take her a full year to complete this special order rug.

Martha Tsosie/36" × 68"

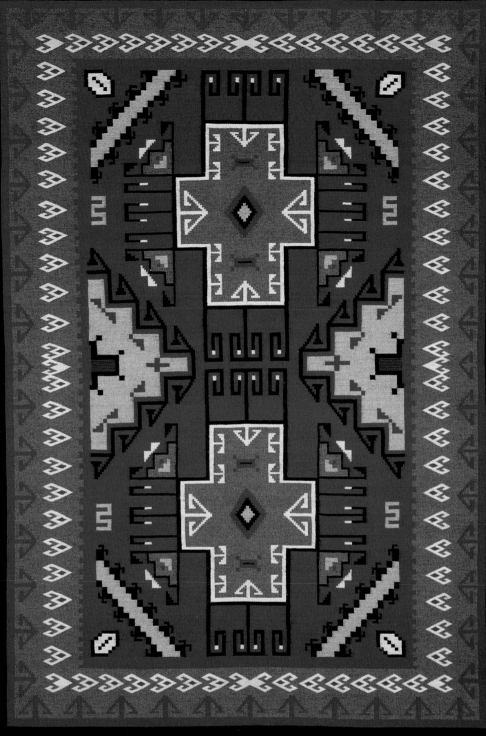

Louise Begay

Louise Begay's rug is an example of a contemporary "chiefs" blanket; these were originally intended as wearing blankets in historic times. This type of rug is popular among Ganado area weavers as it was originally revived there by Lorenzo Hubbell around the turn of the century.

The photo below is of Ray Manley and myself, documenting Alice's and Sadie's Ganado rug for this book.

Sadie Curtis–Alice Balone/4' × 6'

Sadie and Alice

The above rug is an outstanding example of a classic, contemporary Ganado red rug. It combines a deep red background with stylized cross and serrate design elements. There are three colors of natural gray wools used in combination with white and black accents, the overall effect being visually well-balanced and dramatic at the same time.

Crystal

The area of Crystal is nestled on the western slope of the Chuska Mountain range. Having an abundant water supply has made it a fine area for raising livestock and crops. The Navajo term for the area is "Tonlt'ili" meaning "where the crystal water flows out." It has also been established as an area for fine weaving since just before the turn of the century. The rugs for which it was famous originally were aniline-dyed and elaborately designed. It was not until the mid-1940s that the borderless, vegetal-dyed designs that are associated today with the region of Crystal became established.

Marjorie Hardy/4' × 5'

The example by Marie Brown is very reminiscent of the early transitional wearing blankets, both in design and weave.

Marie Brown /5' × 7'

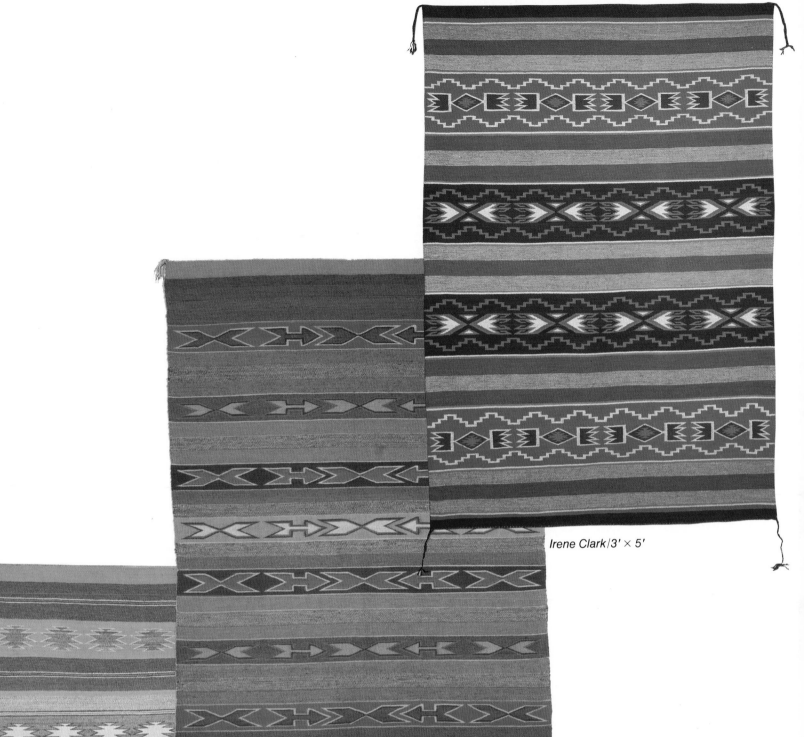

Irene Clark/3' × 5'

Sarah Begay/4' × 6'

This area's style of weaving of today is sometimes confused with the Wide Ruins and Chinle area banded design rugs; it is also a revival of the "early classic period." In this case the design bands are horizontally bordered by the distinctive "wavey line," which is accomplished by simply alternating the color of individual weft strands for a short distance on either side of the geometric design band. Also of note is the more extensive use of the natural wool colors with the vegetal tones. The combination is very pleasing to the eye as well as being compatible with most contemporary decor.

Nanabah Harrison/4' × 6'

Two Grey Hills

Two Grey Hills is located on the east side of the Chuska Mountains. In the early 1900s the weavers in this area were imitating the elaborate and bordered geometric designs developed by trader J. B. Moore in the Crystal area. They reflected an Oriental design influence, and utilized the bright aniline colors which were popular all over the Reservation at this time.

By 1930, through the influence of the area's traders at that time, the use of bright analine colors had been eliminated. The one exception is the use of aniline black, which highlights the natural black sheep's wool. All other colors were those obtained from the carding and combining of natural wools: black wool carded with white to produce varying shades of gray, brown wool with white to produce tans and beiges. Thus has evolved a very distinct regional style, utilizing only these natural wool colors obtained from their native sheep. Many sheep in this area are bred specifically for the color of fleece they will produce.

Alice Gorman/3′ × 5′

By the 1960s the "super-fine" tapestries had evolved. These have weft thread count from ninety to one hundred-thirty per inch, and as many as 25 to 30 warp threads per inch as well. These pieces rank as some of the finest handwoven woolen textiles ever produced anywhere in the world. Also, many months are required to complete a relatively small example. These pieces are generally framed and displayed by their proud owners.

It is not unusual to find several different shades of gray, brown, and tan in a single Two Grey Hills rug or tapestry. Combined with a series of complex geometr designs, they can result in a breath-takingly beautiful work of art. Justifiably, these are some of the finest of all Navajo weavings, and some of the most expensive and highly prized of those produced today.

Rachael and Melvin Curley/30″ × 42″/Tapestry Weave

Daisy Taugelchee/36″ × 60″

The above closeup is a detail of a superfine tapestry by Daisy Taugelchee. It was photographed with a strong light from behind only, and illustrates just how finely the wool had to be carded and spun in order to take on this opaque, translucent quality. The weft count in this particular weaving averages between 125 and 130 per inch. It is truly an outstanding Two Grey Hills tapestry reflecting a capability possessed by only a very small number of Navajo weavers today. Tomorrow?

Virginia Deal/38″ × 60″

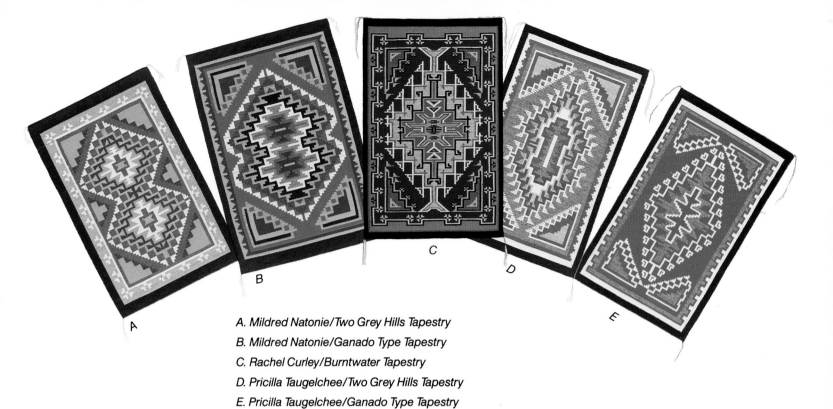

A. Mildred Natonie/Two Grey Hills Tapestry

B. Mildred Natonie/Ganado Type Tapestry

C. Rachel Curley/Burntwater Tapestry

D. Pricilla Taugelchee/Two Grey Hills Tapestry

E. Pricilla Taugelchee/Ganado Type Tapestry

F. Stella Arizana/30″ × 42″/Burntwater Tapestry

G. Mary Lee Begay/3′ × 5′/Two Grey Hills (woven in the Ganado area)

The examples shown above are indications of what is to come in Navajo weaving. No longer will one style be limited to a single area. In the last ten years weavers from all parts of the Reservation have been experimenting with designs, techniques, and color combinations of the other regions of the Navajo Reservation. It reflects a greater awareness and curiosity of the individual weaver and of the possibilities for artistic growth. It is the future of their art form.

Sandpaintings

Weavings depicting Navajo sandpaintings are perhaps the most sought-after product of the native loom. They represent dry paintings which are made of colored sands and are used only for specific curing ceremonies. These ceremonies can be performed solely by the Hatathli, or Medicine man, who has spent many years learning a particular "sing."

Anna Mae Tanner/House of Moving Points/5' × 5'

In the early nineteen twenties a very powerful Medicine man from the Two Grey Hills area began weaving full sandpainting designs into rugs. It was his desire to preserve, for all time, the sandpaintings of some of the important ceremonies that he conducted. His name was Hosteen Klah, or Left Handed Singer. He also instructed two nieces, Gladys and Irene Manuelito, in the art of creating the very intricately detailed designs. Gladys Manuelito taught her daughter-in-law, Ruby, who is still practicing the art today. While it is not clear if Klah was the first to weave a true sandpainting design into a rug, it is probable that he was the first to do so with the accuracy obtained from his life time of training in ceremonial knowledge.

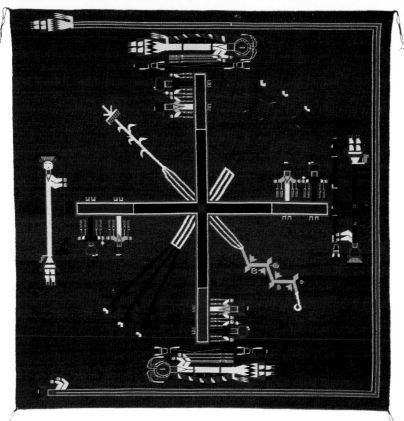

Ruby Manuelito/Whirling Logs/42″ × 42″ Tapestry

Today there are still only a very few Navajo weavers who are willing and/or capable of producing these highly symbolic images of their ceremonial heritage. They require tremendous patience and technical ability on the part of the artist. It is also necessary, they feel, that special ceremonial sings be conducted to protect these individuals from spiritual harm.

Rugs with sandpainting designs have been produced in several different parts of the Reservation. Still the ones with the finest weaves and most accurate designs (none is completely accurate, intentionally) are produced in the Two Grey Hills and Shiprock areas. Their production is very limited, and they are eagerly sought by museums and collectors. Sandpainting rugs are the rarest and most valuable of all Navajo textiles.

Mary Long/Feather People/5′ × 5′

Anna Mae Tanner/Buffalo Never Dies/5′ × 5′

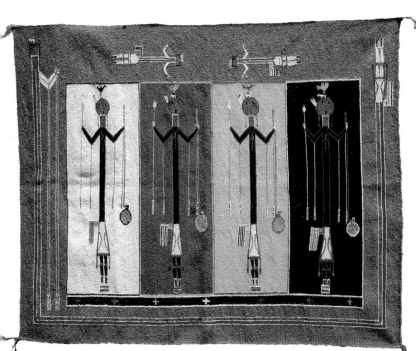

Ruby Manuelito/House of Six Directions/28″ × 34″ Tapestry

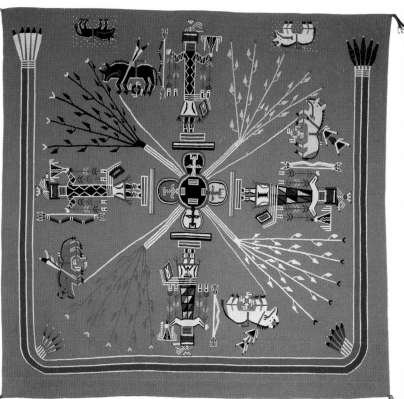

Teec Nos Pos

Teec Nos Pos, or Circle of Cottonwoods, is located on the north side of the Carrizo Mountains, near the four corners area. The weaving here displays a strong Persian influence—and has since the early 1900s. This is probably due to photographs of such rugs being circulated among the weavers, by traders, for design ideas. Perhaps a broader diversity of materials is used in this weaving than anywhere else on the Reservation. Everything from handspun natural wool colors to brightly colored commercial yarns are combined in very intricately designed and, in general, very well woven rugs. Even vegetal dyed wools are used to a limited extent, with very pleasing results.

It is this broad diversity of materials combined with the very intricate design work that give the Teec Nos Pos such great appeal to collectors.

Helen Begay/4' × 7'/Homespun Native Wool

Alice Begay/4' × 6'/Vegetal Dye

A. Alice Nelson/6' × 9'

B. Marie Wallace/5' × 8'

C. Bessie George/4' × 7'

D. Mary Tom/3' × 4'/Red Mesa Outline Teec Nos Pos

A.

B.

C.

D.

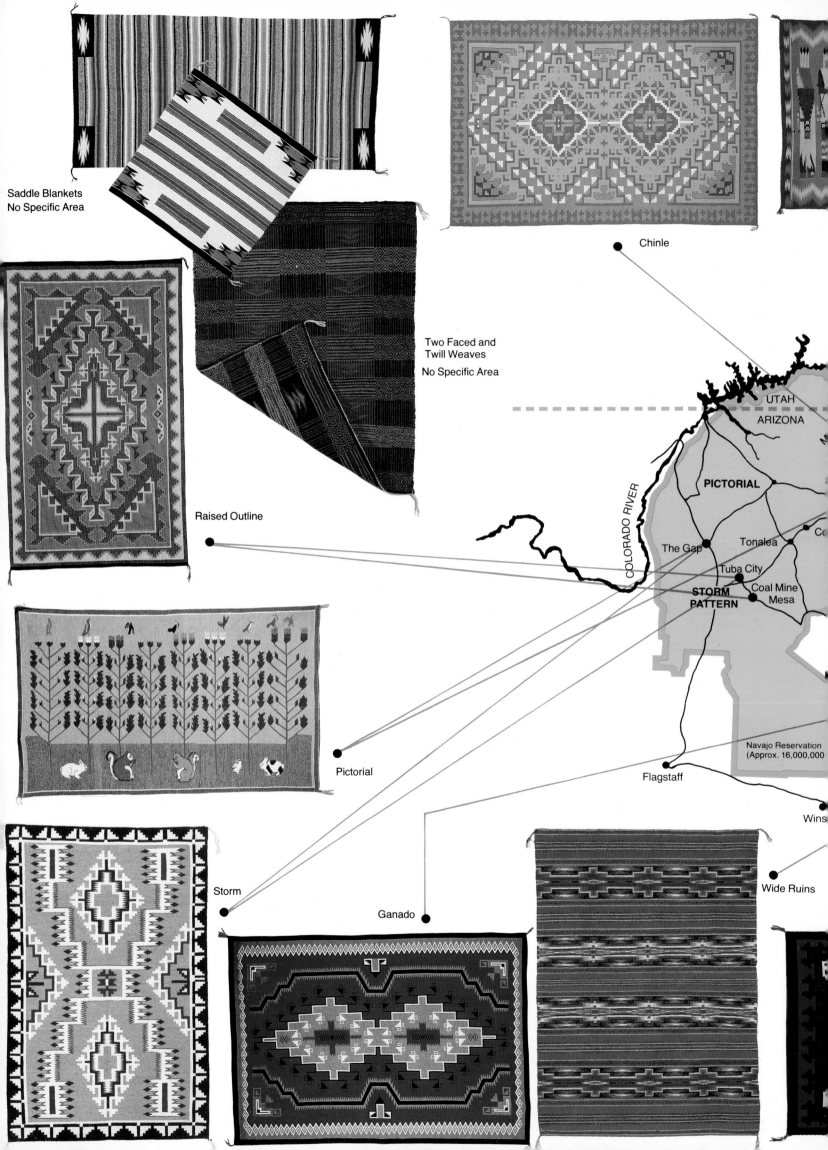

Saddle Blankets
No Specific Area

Two Faced and
Twill Weaves

No Specific Area

Raised Outline

Pictorial

Storm

Ganado

Chinle

UTAH
ARIZONA

COLORADO RIVER

PICTORIAL

The Gap

Tonalea

Tuba City

Coal Mine
Mesa

STORM
PATTERN

Navajo Reservation
(Approx. 16,000,000

Flagstaff

Wins

Wide Ruins

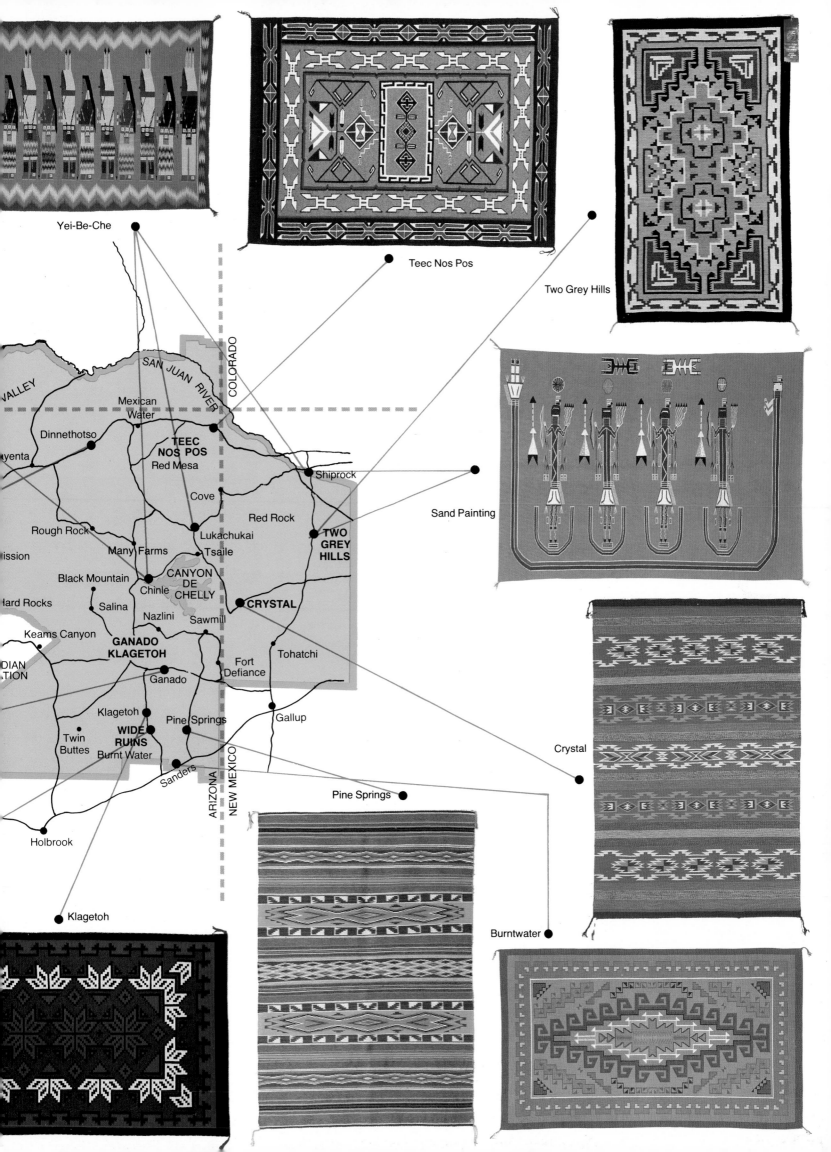

Yei-Be-Che

Teec Nos Pos

Two Grey Hills

COLORADO

SAN JUAN RIVER

VALLEY

Mexican Water

Dinnethotso

Kayenta

TEEC NOS POS

Red Mesa

Shiprock

Sand Painting

Cove

Rough Rock

Red Rock

Lukachukai

TWO GREY HILLS

Many Farms

Tsaile

Mission

Black Mountain

CANYON DE CHELLY

Chinle

Hard Rocks

Salina

CRYSTAL

Nazlini

Sawmill

Keams Canyon

GANADO KLAGETOH

Fort Defiance

Tohatchi

Crystal

INDIAN RESERVATION

Ganado

Klagetoh

Pine Springs

Gallup

Twin Buttes

WIDE RUINS

Burnt Water

Sanders

ARIZONA

NEW MEXICO

Pine Springs

Burntwater

Holbrook

Klagetoh

Pictorials

Prehistoric Indian Petroglyph

Desba Jake/3' x 4'/ This one is most unusual, it shows a Hopi Basket Dance with masked Kachinas. This weaver lives in the vicinity of the Hopi Mesas and has probably attended this dance.

From the fertile imagination of the Navajo weaver has sprung a category of rugs known as Pictorials. They can be anything from day to day observations of Navajo life to the repetition of slogans or sayings (my favorite so far being "God Bless Cowboys and Indians"). They can depict anything from a Navajo ceremony to fanciful wildlife scenes. Absolutely anything is possible.

While this style of weaving is not limited to any one sector of the Navajo Reservation, my observations have been that they are more common in the north-central and north-western areas, possibly because these sections do not have a set style of their own and have had to borrow from others for ideas.

Pictorials have long been considered by many to be true expressions of "Navajo Folk Art," and have a great following among collectors who do not necessarily desire the other types of Navajo weavings.

Since before the turn of the century, when a weaver decided to document in wool her impression of the first train or automobile she saw, Pictorials have been a hit.

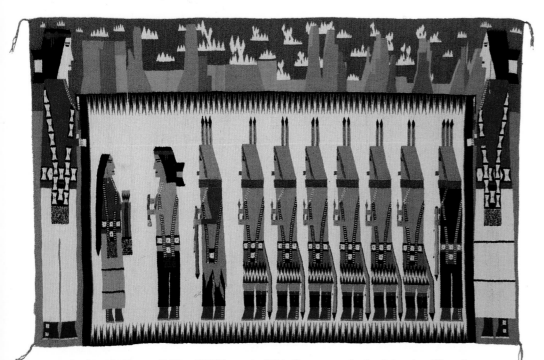

Della Woody Begay/30" × 38"/Tapestry/This fine example depicts a traditionally dressed Navajo man and woman holding up a rug of a Yei-Be-Che ceremony.

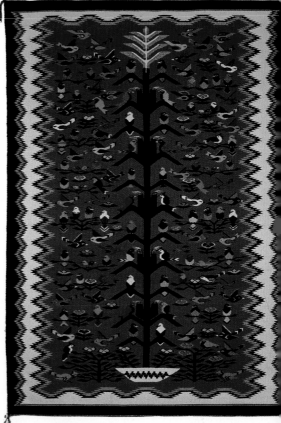

Evelyn Tunney/4' × 6'

Linda Nez/3½' × 5'/ "Traditional Navajo Reservation Life."

   A Pictorial rug of exceptional quality depicting traditional Navajo Reservation life and scenery. The man on the left is doing silverwork in front of the hogan, or traditional Navajo home. The grandmother and granddaughter are grinding corn while seated on a sheepskin. The corn meal is then placed in the Navajo basket beside them. The other two women are carding and spinning wool for the rug they are weaving.

Elain Bia/5' × 7'/represents the 2nd day of a Navajo squaw dance (Enemy Way Ceremony). This is a three day ceremony.

Storm Pattern

The areas of the Western Reservation between Tuba City and Tonalea (Where the Water Comes Together) are where the Storm pattern is predominantly woven. It first appeared sometime around the turn of the century, and probably could be attributed to a trader's visual conception of a Navajo legend. It is also said to have first appeared on flour sacks from Flagstaff about that time.

A. Mary Wilson Begay/4' × 6'

B. Marie Sheppard/4' × 6'

A.

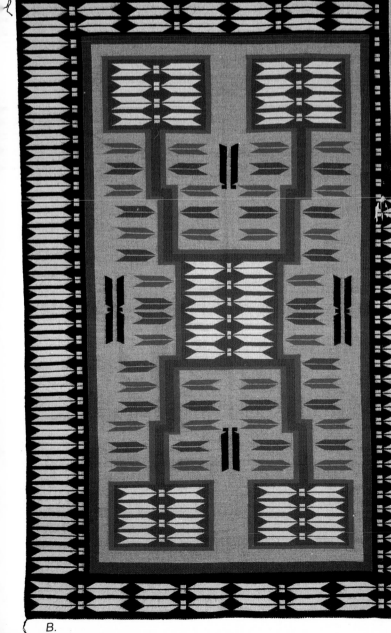

B.

Some say that the complex design elements of this rug are highly symbolic. There is a box at the geometric center of the rug which is said to represent the spiritual center of the Navajo universe. From the center, four zig-zagging lines (representing lightning bolts) radiate to boxes in each quadrant or corner. These are said to represent the homes or "hogans" of the four winds, or four directions or four sacred mountains bordering the Navajo World. In between these are geometric designs representing water symbols (water bugs and clouds) or swastikas, which represent whirling logs. It is not unusual, also, to see designs representing sacred feathers and bows and arrows. Originally, the colors used were red, black, and white with a natural gray or red background. They now can be seen in natural browns and vegetal dye colors. They can also be found in many other areas of the Reservation, but not in any significant quantity.

The complexity of the design combined with all of the possible symbolism has made this type of rug popular with collectors.

A. Monument Valley

B. Ason Begay / Four In One / 4' × 6'

C. Mabel Bighorse / 5' × 7'

Yeis and Yei-Be-Ches

Susie Yazzie is weaving while her mother-in-law spins wool for her.

Betty Bia (deceased) wove this top quality Yei-Be-Che/3' x 7'.

Yeis

A Yei is a stylized figure of a Navajo deity which has been adapted from the sandpainting designs of the religious healing ceremonies. When used in the rug context, however, it is symbolic, but has no specific religious meaning. These designs first began appearing in the Shiprock area around 1910, once again, most likely at the encouragement of an area trader. Today this style of weaving can be found in limited quantity throughout the Reservation.

The three major areas for this style of weaving are located on the northeastern and northwestern sides of the Chuska Mountains. They are Shiprock, Lukachukai, and Chinle. The rugs from the Shiprock area tend to be smaller, and they are finely woven from brightly colored commercial yarns which are supplied by traders in that area. They also tend toward the use of fewer Yei figures and more filler designs, particularly of feathers and cornstalks. The Yei type rugs woven in the Lukachukai-Chinle area tend more toward the natural earth tones of the native wools and vegetal dye combinations. In all areas it is common to see the Yei figures surrounded by the guardian rainbow Yei symbol.

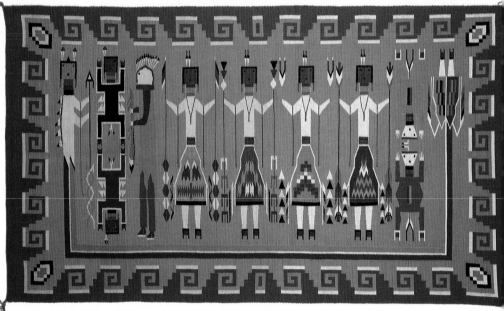

Marie Brown /3' × 5'/Vegetal dye with sandpainting elements.

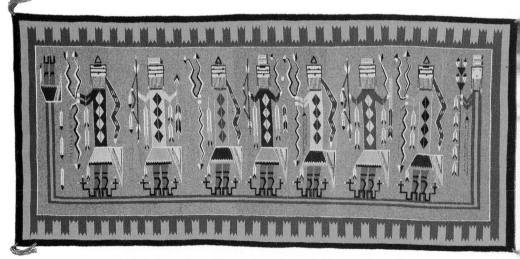

Mary Chase/Approx. 30" × 60"/Native wool, with sandpainting elements.

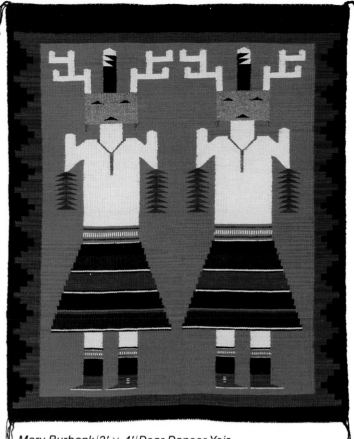

Mary Burbank/3' × 4'/Dear Dancer Yeis

Yei-Be-Ches

(Spiritual Grandfathers) Grandfathers of the gods

This type of rug design represents the human personification of the Yei or deities. They are participants in a Navajo healing ceremony known as the NightWay Chant.

When woven into rugs the Yei-Be-Ches are most often shown dancing in profile. Generally there are from eight to ten Yei-Be-Ches with a leader, and they are followed by the clown or watersprinkler. Some examples are done with both male and female Yei figures dancing while the medicine man or Hatathli administers to a patient holding a Navajo Medicine basket. Due to the tremendous amount of detail and the very sensitive spiritual nature of the ceremonial subject matter, relatively few of these weavings are produced; most of these woven are done in the Shiprock area.

Velma Begay/3' × 5'/Vegetal dye

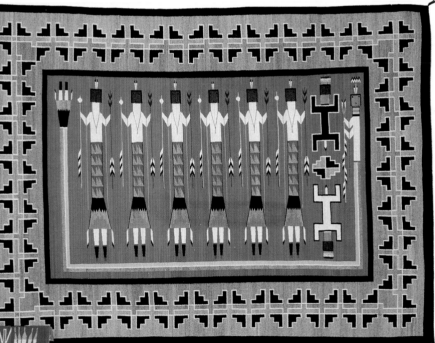

Marie Brown /5' × 7'/Hand carded native wool

During the annual Navajo Shiprock fair, held in October, the first Yei-Be-Che dance of the season is performed, thus marking the beginning of the Yei-Be-Che season. This important nine day ceremony may be performed only during the winter months.

Nazlini—Chinle—Manyfarms

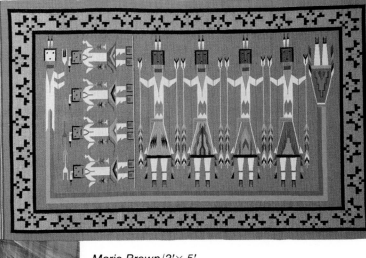

Marie Brown/3' × 5'

Canyon De Chelly

Isabell Johns/30" × 36"/Many Farms Pictorial

Ruth Ann Tracey/4' × 6'

Chinle
(it flows from the canyon)

The Chinle area type of weaving probably best exemplifies the breakdown in a regional style. Located in the geographic center of the Navajo Reservation, it is a crossroads for travel and commerce from one part to another. Also, in recent years there has been little input or interest shown by traders of this area for this weaving.

During the late 1920s and early 1930s, a far-sighted trader by the name of Leon H (Cozy) McSparron was responsible for establishing a new regional style of weaving, the Chinle. This involved the revival of the borderless and banded designs of the Early Classic Period of Navajo weaving (1700–1850) and the bordered red, gray, black, and white of the Ganado type inspired by Lorenzo Hubbell, who had traded in this area from 1900–1919. This new Chinle style still reflected some Hubbell influence: while the design bands were basically done in vegetal dyes, there was some retention of the use of aniline red and black for highlights. The Chinle style became popular immediately and so continued to evolve.

Grace Brown/4' × 6'/Chinle design with natural grey and brown wools with vegetal dyes

Marie Brown/4' × 5'/aniline red with vegetal dye

Helen Bia 4' × 6'

Some people feel that these designs too closely resemble those of the Wide Ruins and Crystal types. The fact is that the Chinle style provided the inspiration for and preceded the transitions in these areas by ten and twenty years, respectively.

Today the Chinle style of weaving is produced in limited quantities and is giving way to the popular types of other areas. This is primarily due to the lack of a market and interest by traders to buy these rugs. Instead, it is necessary for the weaver to travel many miles in all directions to find a market for her work. Then she is required to reproduce the styles of these other areas to receive the best prices. These circumstances have established the most versatile group of weaving artists to be found anywhere on the Reservation. A similar situation exists in the sub-areas of Nazlini (It Flows Around) to the south and Many Farms to the north.

Canyon De Chelly

Specialty Weavings

Of special interest to the advanced collector of contemporary Navajo textiles are some of the examples shown here. They represent the unique and unusual, and demonstrate once again the imagination and talents of some of the more advanced weaving artists. The more expert weavers are constantly seeking new challenges and attempting to learn novel approaches in order to sustain artistic growth, in addition to improving their incomes.

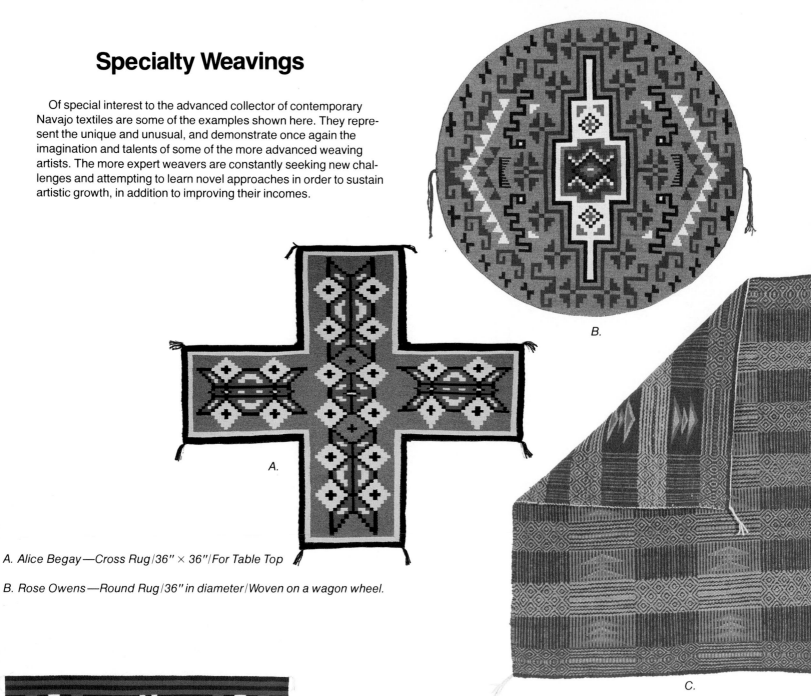

A.

B.

C.

A. Alice Begay—Cross Rug/36" × 36"/For Table Top

B. Rose Owens—Round Rug/36" in diameter/Woven on a wagon wheel.

C. Martha Yazzie/30" × 40"/Two-Faced Rug

D. Helen Scott/4' × 6'/Contemporary Chief Blanket; Moki design

E. Mary Johnson/4' × 6'/Contemporary Germantown Reproduction

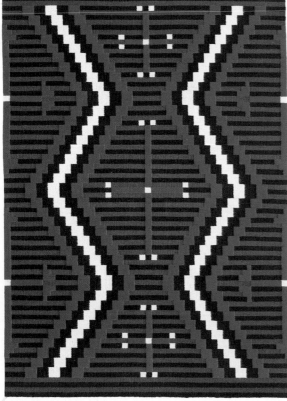

D.

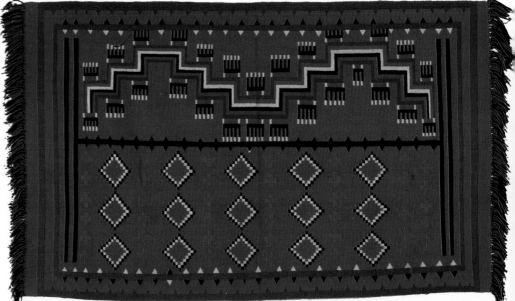

E.

The above example of a four-in-one tapestry by Anna Mae Tanner is the finest example I've yet seen. It combines four distinctly different styles of designing, each being accurately executed as if it had been done by four separate top artists of these particular areas. In 1977 Anna Mae traded this rug for a new pick-up truck and "dó ba ah beso," "with some money on top."

The weaving by Marie Brown on the right is an exceptional "rug in a rug" type. The center Burntwater design is complete, again down to the addition of corner tassels. When I first saw this rug only the bottom design band had been completed, and that was inspired by Mera's book on pueblo embroidery designs with which I had supplied her; also, at my suggestion, she continued the design up vertically to border the central Burntwater pattern which I also requested. The results were quite pleasing as well as unique.

Miniature Rugs

Miniature Loom by Catherine Cleveland

In recent years a new interest in the collecting of Indian art has evolved, namely that of miniatures. A few Navajo weavers have ably answered the call. They are capable of producing nearly every style of weaving in miniature. The finest examples are woven in the Fort Defiance area. Generally they are made of respun commercial yarns and are of tapestry quality.

Miniatures

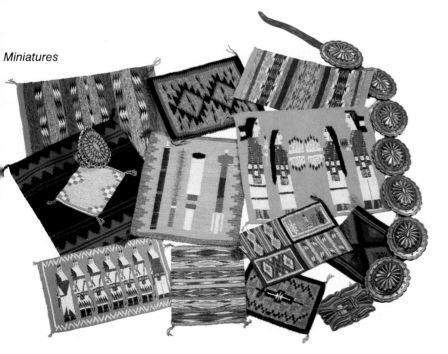

Raised Outline

This unique style of weaving involves a special technique which results in a three dimensional effect known as a raised outline. The designs are outlined in two alternating colors which are slighlty raised on one side of the rug. This is done through a manipulation of the warp and weft threads, thus creating this unusual effect. This raised outlining of the pattern appears only on the front side, giving each side a distinctively different visual appearance with the same design. It was developed in the Western Reservation areas of Coal Mine Mesa and Tuba City in the 1950s, and is still primarily done in these regions.

Jeane Begay/57" × 62"/Burntwater design

Marie Watson/44" × 66"/Ganado Type

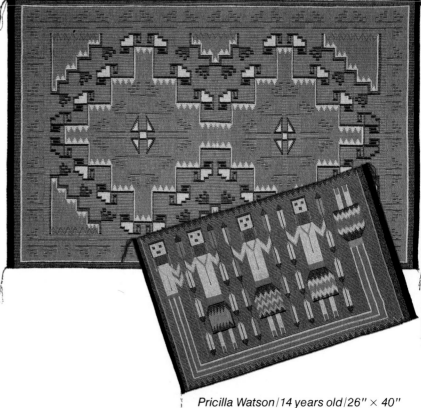

Marie Watson/4' × 7'/Two Grey Hills Type

Pricilla Watson/14 years old/26" × 40"

A Perspective on Collecting and Living With Navajo Weaving

Ones surroundings can be greatly enhanced by the collecting of Navajo rugs. They may be used in a special room or throughout ones home—or they may be stored in a treasure chest. Perhaps the greatest satisfaction comes from daily living with these pieces, on the floor, sometimes with several hanging on the wall. Again color can be played with to the individual's satisfaction. Black and white plus soft grays and tans of the Two Gray Hills styles might satisfy one who prefers less color; however, the best of these would be of too fine a weave, therefore too precious for floor use. The many colors derived from endless desert plants softly blended in Chinle and Wide Ruins vegetal dye rugs could be used in the most modern of homes, with many of the sturdier of these pieces serving most effectively as rugs. Then there is the collector who so enjoys Navajo rugs that he uses them throughout his home, and has some "extras" stacked away in a closet. The former he enjoys daily, consciously and unconsciously; the latter he shares with those friends who share with him the pleasures of fine craftsmanship and creative design.

Thus the individual can have his private collection, to be used or not to be used, but always to be cherished. He can spend a little or much money on it, and it can become dearer to him through the years, both monetarily and esthetically.

by Clara Lee Tanner, in Ray Manley's Collecting Southwestern Indian Arts & Crafts

Today there are several fine galleries dealing exclusively in superior quality Indian art located around the country. This attractive display is from a prominent Scottsdale gallery.

Imagine the impression created upon entry into this fine home.

The weavers of this Teec Nos Pos rug live in the vicinity of Shiprock, New Mexico. It is a most unusual design and one might wonder how such a strong pattern might fit into a modern home. The fine workmanship of a quality craft seems to always find a natural blending with any decor.

After purchasing this exceptional Ganado red rug by Sadie Curtis, this proud collector decided to design and redecorate this entire room around it.

A Two Grey Hills tapestry is woven with more than 120 wefts to the inch. Though they are often framed, this one graces a formal dining room table.

This unique decor is from a Tucson attorney's office.

Contemporary vegetal dye weaving is amazingly versatile and compatible with any decor. This is illustrated here in comfortable combination with fine Victorian era furnishings.

The Kiva (ceremonial chamber) shown here was designed and built specifically to display this outstanding collection of Indian art. This collector is proud to display one or more of each of the defined area weavings plus pottery, baskets and kachinas from some of the best Hopi artists.

Ganado reds make this bedroom warm and comfortable. To live with functional art gives double satisfaction.

Rugs 8 by 10 feet in size are rare, but a few great ones are still woven. This Ganado red by Mary Lee Begay and the smaller Two Grey Hills create a beautiful library setting.

Historic Blankets

Early Classic Period (1700–1840)

It is now widely believed that the Navajo have been weaving for the last three hundred years, and quite possibly longer. This is contrary to the long-held opinion that they learned the art from the Rio Grande Pueblo Indians who sought refuge with them in the years following the great Pueblo Revolt against the Spanish in 1680. Designs of this era were simple banded patterns done primarily in natural wool colors. They learned also the use of indigo, which was traded from the Spanish. Even at this early date a reputation for the quality of Navajo blankets had begun to spread as they were traded among the early settlers and other neighboring Indians. These fabrics were intended for hard everyday use and often were worn to nothing or they were interred with their owners at the time of death, so very few examples of this era remain for study.

Navajo woven dress, circa 1870

Serape, circa 1860

Chiefs Blanket 2nd phase, circa 1890

Classic Period (1840–1863)

By this time the Navajo had achieved a level of excellence in their weaving that was unsurpassed by anything produced by their Pueblo and Mexican neighbors. The products of their native loom were highly prized and extensively traded to other Indians and Anglos alike.

This period marks a high point of their technical spinning and weaving abilities. This was brought about by the extensive use of red baize or bayeta yarns raveled and respun from bolts of European cloth for which they traded, and the necessity to match its fine and even consistency when respun and used with their own native wools. The deep red cochineal and lac-dyed wools added a new dimension to their weaving when combined with indigo, natural wool, and vegetal colors. Also available through trade were the fine and colorful three-ply yarns known as Saxony, so named for their German origin. All these factors made for extremely fine weavings of consistently high quality.

Along with the newly expanded color palette came new concepts for design. Diamonds and crosses, serrate and terraced patterns were introduced and became quite popular. This was also a period of great demand, with blankets of exceptional quality commanding substantial sums and ranking in quality and value with the famous Saltillo serapes of Colonial Mexico. This era of prosperity came to a sudden and traumatic close in 1863. The Navajo people were rounded up and incarcerated by the United States Government at Bosque Redondo in central New Mexico in reprisal for their incessant raiding on the neighboring Mexican, American, and Pueblo settlements. Unable to obtain their native wools for five years, while in captivity, the Navajo turned solely to the use of machine-made yarns. These were supplied by their captors in exchange for blankets woven in addition to all manner of trade goods. (The blankets on pages 44–45, of later date, are representative of earlier styles.)

Transitional wearing blanket, circa 1890

Childs wearing blanket, circa 1870

Transitional Period (1863–1890)

The proud Navajo people were allowed to return to their homelands in 1868, this being at first a difficult re-adjustment to Reservation life. In the past they had been fiercely independent of all others. They were now forced to adjust to the Anglo culture and progressively increased dependence on the U.S. government for this new way of life. This was accomplished with very little incident as Navajos wanted only to be able to remain in their beloved red rock country within their four sacred mountains.

Now totally familiar with the use of commercial yarns, they began to experiment further with design and color combinations. Patterns became more complex and color combinations more daring. By the mid 1880s the finer imported Saxony and bayeta wools were being replaced by a coarser three- and four-ply yarn called Germantown. This yarn was less expensive and more readily available as most of it was manufactured in Pennsylvania. The height of the Germantown period (1890–1900) also marked a general decline in the overall quality of weaving. This was also a period of transition of the use of Navajo textiles, namely that of wearing blanket to floor covering. With the introduction of commercial fabrics and the Pendleton blanket by traders it became less profitable and less fashionable for the Navajo to weave for themselves. Weaving designs were no longer influenced by the proud image the blanket presented when draped gracefully about the shoulders of its owner, but by the trader who sought new markets for the pieces taken in trade with the Navajo. The era of the rug was born.

Transitional wearing blanket, circa 1880

Germantown, circa 1890

Moki style wearing blanket, circa 1880

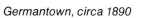

Old and historic weavings courtesy of the Dewald collection

The Rug to Regional Period (1890–1940)

By 1890 it was clearly up to the trader to establish new outlets for weaving if he and the Navajo were to prosper in their dealings together. Several enterprising traders set about marketing a new concept in Navajo weaving, that of rugs for the floor. Weavers were encouraged to work in larger sizes with a heavier weave and to incorporate borders into the patterns. High quality aniline dyes had become readily available in a wide range of colors from traders throughout the Reservation. These were used in combination with home spun wool to create the colorful and durable rug of this time. With the exception of Germantown yarns, most other prespun wools had lost favor for reasons of price and availability. The Eastern demand for the Navajo rug was tremendous.

Two of the most notable traders of this time were Lorenzo Hubbell of Ganado, and J. B. Moore of Crystal. Both men developed their own distinctive style of rug patterns and insisted upon top quality work from their weavers' looms.

J. B. Moore produced a color brochure illustrating the range of patterns, sizes, quality, and price of the rugs that could be "special ordered" from him. In addition to designing his rugs, he would send away the best wools he traded from the Navajo to be commercially cleaned and aniline dyed. Upon their return he would commission the better weavers of his area to spin them and weave them with selected patterns and color combinations. These first measures of quality control were effective and fruitful. The rugs he sold were considered to be some of the finest available.

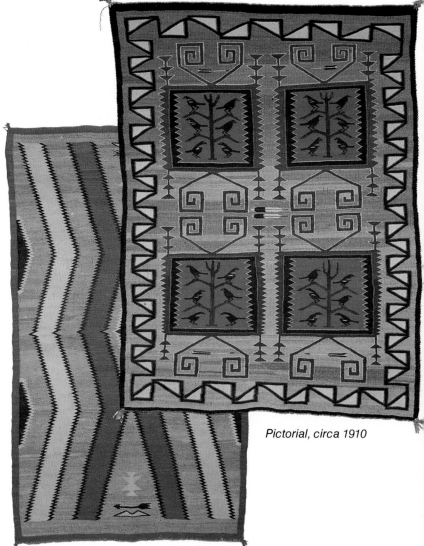

Pictorial, circa 1910

Chinle–Ganado, circa 1910

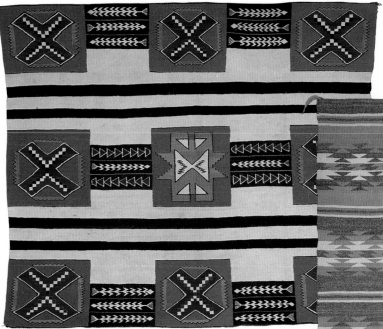

Chiefs style rug, circa 1920

Trader Lorenzo Hubbell had a great influence on this early rug market as well. His influence resulted in one of the first regional styles of Navajo weaving. The rug he designed was a combination of some of the earlier blanket motifs set against a rich red background and then framed with a black border. The distinctively deep red of some of the better rugs was achieved by a process of double-dying the wool; these rugs were unlike any other made at the time. The style endured and remains in favor today.

Wide Ruin (Lippencott Pink), circa 1940

J. B. Moore Style Crystal, circa 1910

Yei-Be-Che, circa 1910

Teec Nos Pos, circa 1930

Two Grey Hills, circa 1920

Ganado–Klagetoh, circa 1940

Fred Harvey

This was also a time of great interest in the "now tamed" western territories of America. Their scenic wonders attracted much tourism even then. The Fred Harvey Co. built their famous "Harvey House" hotel facilities all along the newly completed Santa Fe Railroad, thereby making it possible for people to see the west in style. The most famous facility was built on the south rim of the Grand Canyon. By 1900 the canyon was attracting thousands of the curious annually. Today it is visited by several million tourists annually. This tremendous exposure, combined with Mr. Harvey's own enthusiasm for marketing and collecting fine examples of Navajo textiles and other Indian art, led to a longstanding business relationship with several prominent traders who supplied the quality rugs that stocked the "Harvey House" outlets.

From this time forward various types of rugs would begin to emerge from all areas of the Reservation. If they were favorably received by the buyers, the trader would encourage more such examples. Those which proved hard to sell were discouraged. Through this type of trial and error marketing the distinct styles which are attributed to the different regions of the Navajo Reservation were eventually established. In all cases these styles of weaving have evolved from a local need of the trader to help his areas Navajo customers convert their crafts to cash.

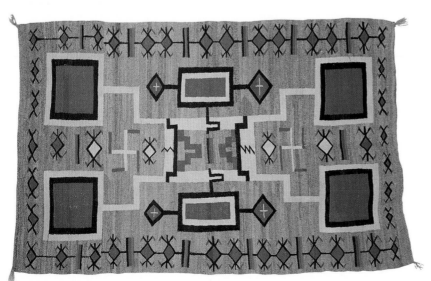

Storm Pattern, circa 1910

(continued from page 1)

Considering that the size of the Navajo Reservation is some sixteen million acres, and the number of jobs available is limited, weaving is a tremendously important source of income for these basically pastoral people. It is not at all uncommon for the women who weave to be the principal bread winner of the family. This accords her considerable prestige within the family and community as well. Traders will extend credit against the rugs of their area's weavers. Through past experience with these artists they have come to know about what to expect of their work, and how much credit to extend against it. Arrangements of this type are the only way it is feasible for most weavers to attempt the more time-consuming pieces, and still meet monthly obligations.

Most of the recognized rug styles of Navajo weaving were established in their respective regions from about 1900 to 1940. These were the Ganado-Klagetoh, Storm pattern, Teec Nos Pos, Shiprock-Lukachukai Yeis, Two Grey Hills, the Chinle, and Wide Ruins-Pine Springs types. The modern vegetal dyed Crystal, Raised Outline, Pictorial, and Burntwater types and regions have been developed since then.

Until the last few decades, the weaver was limited to dealing with the trader of her immediate area. He knew the approximate wealth in livestock and jewelry of all his customers, and what to expect seasonally in the way of lambs, wool, and rugs. Against these assets he would extend credit from his trading post store. It was in the trader's best interest to help his customers profit in their business dealings with him as much as possible, for the more the people could earn, the more they could spend with him. So it was with the weaving as well. In order to market these rugs it was necessary to establish a style which was easily recognized and attributed to an individual trader or area of the Reservation. The lack of adequate transportation, poor road conditions, and great distances between trading posts also helped to cement this bond between Navajo and trader.

In recent years, a gradual "breakdown" of this adherance to individual regional styles has developed. This began with the addition of the pick-up truck to the Navajo lifestyle. Diné (The People) love to travel to all areas of the homeland, attending ceremonies and fairs, visiting and helping relatives while gaining perspective on the issues of these areas. With this exposure has come the desire to experiment with the other styles of weaving and to broaden their market. A weaver might travel several hundred miles trying many different buyers in order to be sure of receiving the best price for her work.

Along with this increased mobility there has developed a decreased dependency on the trading post. Major marketing and convenience store chains are springing up across the Reservation. The small trading posts, unable to compete because of higher overhead (shipping cost), are being forced out of business. Sadly, many of these older trading posts have been destroyed by vandalism and fire shortly after closing. Some of the picturesque older posts represent an important era in the history and development of the Navajo tribe and should be developed and preserved. It is important to note that without the trader, Navajo weaving most probably would be a lost art. At the very least, it could never have evolved into what it is today.

Another important factor contributing to the overall increase in the quality of the weaving, during the last few decades, has been the availability of processed wools. This began in the 1960s as a Navajo wool project by the tribe. Wool and mohair would be purchased from the people to be sent away for cleaning and processing then the better grades were sold back to the weavers. This wool was particularly well suited to vegetal dye work as it was cleaner than was generally possible when done by hand, and would take the plants dyes more consistently.

Susie Yazzie, Monument Valley

In the last two hundred years Navajo weaving has come a long way: from the shoulder, to the floor, to a place of distinction on the gallery wall. Each weaving is not simply a technical representation of a craft but an individual expression in a visual and touchable art form. Many Navajo artists have distinct styles and their weaving reveals a unique quality in fineness, color, and theme. With our support the art of this unique Southwestern people will continue to evolve, delight, and educate us for many years to come.

SUGGESTED READING

Amsden, Charles. *Navajo Weaving.* 2nd ed. Albuquerque: University of New Mexico Press, 194?
Bryan, Nonabah G. and Stella Young. *Navajo Native Dyes: Their Preparation and Use.* Reprint. Palmer Lake, Colorado: Filter Press, 1980.
Dedera, Don. *Navajo Rugs.* Flagstaff, Arizona: Northland Press, 1975.
Dutton, Bertha P. *Navajo Weaving Today.* Santa Fe: Museum of New Mexico Press, 1961.
Fox, Nancy. *Pueblo Weaving and Textile Arts.* Santa Fe: Museum of New Mexico, 1979.
Kent, Kate Peck. *Navajo Weaving.* Phoenix, Arizona: Heard Museum, 1961.